HIDE & SEEK SCIENCE

Where's That Spider?

by Barbara Brenner and Bernice Chardiet

Illustrated by Carol Schwartz

Cartwheel
B·O·O·K·S®

SCHOLASTIC INC.

NEW YORK   TORONTO   LONDON   AUCKLAND   SYDNEY
MEXICO CITY   NEW DELHI   HONG KONG

To Jane and Margaret Chardiet
—B.C.

To Ed and Ruth
—C.S.

Text copyright © 1999 by Barbara Brenner and Bernice Chardiet.
Illustrations copyright © 1999 by Carol Schwartz.
All rights reserved. Published by Scholastic Inc.
SCHOLASTIC, CARTWHEEL BOOKS and the CARTWHEEL BOOKS logo
are trademarks and/or registered trademarks of Scholastic Inc.
HIDE & SEEK SCIENCE is a trademark of Chardiet Unlimited, Inc.

ISBN 0-590-12818-3

12 11 10 9 8 7 6 5 4   0/0 01 02 03 04
Printed in the U.S.A.   14
First printing, September 1999

Introduction

Look in that web.
Look in that hole.
Watch for eyes
As black as coal.

Look on leaves.
Look in the air.
Can you see them?
Where? Where? Where?

The Spiders Are Landing!

What's going on here?
Suddenly the air is filled with threads of silk.
Each thread has a tiny spider on it.
Some of the spiders have already landed!
Can you find ten new arrivals in the grass?

It's a Fact:
Most young spiders find their new homes
by "ballooning."
They launch into the air and land a few
yards or many miles from where they
were born.
Airplane pilots have seen ballooning spiders
more than two miles up in the air!

Spiders in the Attic

This spooky old attic has lots of cobwebs.
And cobwebs are made by — spiders!
There are two of them living here.
They're hiding near their webs,
waiting for insects to get trapped.
Then they'll run out and kill the insects
with their poison fangs!
Can you find these two tiny killers?

It's a Fact:
The house spider (also called sheetweb spider)
is the spider you usually see in homes and garages.
Its web looks something like a flat sheet.
This spider weaves special trip lines
in the web to trap its prey.
Why doesn't the spider get its own legs caught?
Now that's a mystery!

Prowlers in the Woods

There's a wolf spider prowling these woods.
It's searching for a juicy grasshopper
or millipede to eat.
But there's another prowler overhead—
a hunting wasp.
The wasp is looking for a wolf spider
to feed its young.
The wolf spider's hole is nearby.
Do you see it?
Do you think the wolf spider can get back
home in time?

It's a Fact:
Wolf spiders don't make webs.
Instead, they chase their prey and run it down,
the way wolves do.
That's where they get their name.
Wolf spiders often prowl in the dark.
They have eight eyes to help them see.
Hunting wasps are their greatest enemies.

Crab Spider Camouflage

Any bee or butterfly that visits this flower
is in for a nasty surprise.
There's a crab spider inside,
ready to deliver a deadly bite.
Can you find it?

It's a Fact:
Crab spiders scuttle sideways just like crabs.
They hide in flowers and plants.
They attack with a poison bite on an insect's
neck or head.
A crab spider can change color to match
the flower it's hiding in.
One kind of crab spider hides on bananas.
Guess what color it is.

Beware! Black Widow!

Here's a black widow spider. WATCH OUT!
This lady carries powerful poison.
Sometimes she kills her mate and then eats him!
But there's a male black widow in this scene
who seems willing to take a chance.
Do you see the brave male spider?

It's a Fact:
Almost all spiders carry venom.
But the female black widow spider of the
southern United States is famous for hers.
Although she is only about half an inch long,
her poison has occasionally killed humans.
Luckily, the black widow isn't usually
found near people.

Cartwheel in the Garden

This orange garden spider has just finished
weaving its web.
And now here comes a tiny moth!
When the moth lands, the spider will feel
the vibration on its web.
But the spider can't see the moth. Can you?

It's a Fact:
Garden spiders spin cartwheel-shaped webs,
sometimes called orb webs.
The silk comes from six tiny spinnerets
at the end of the spider's belly.
This spider can spin different thicknesses of silk.
Some of the silk is sticky so the spider
can catch its prey.
But the orange garden spider never gets stuck.
It has a coating of oil on its legs!

Spider Mom

Female tarantulas may *look* mean and fierce.
But they are good spider moms.
They don't let their young ones out of their sight.
See those round cocoons that these two spiders are carrying?
They're full of spider eggs. But — oops!
One spider has dropped her cocoon.
She's looking all around.
Can you help her find it?

It's a Fact:
Female tarantulas and many other spiders
carry their cocoons with them.
After the baby spiders hatch out,
the female may carry them on her back for a while.
If one spider baby falls off,
Mom quickly retrieves it.

Which Is the Spider, Which Is the Ant?

There's a stranger marching in this parade of ants.
It *looks* like an ant.
It seems to wiggle its antennae like an ant.
But, is it an ant?
Can you find this pretender?

It's a Fact:
The ant-mimic spider hides among ants.
It even imitates the actions of ants.
Scientists think this spider mimics ants
because ants taste bad.
They're avoided by creatures that eat spiders.
So, if the spider looks like an ant,
it has a better chance to stay alive!

A Giant of a Spider

There's a hairy giant loose in the jungle tonight!
Right now this silent stalker has its eyes on
the hummingbird.
Can you see the giant crawling up the tree?
Let's hope the hummingbird can see it.

It's a Fact:
The hairy South American bird spider
is a monster of the tarantula family.
One species is ten inches long from toe to toe —
as big as a dinner plate!
This spider eats lizards, birds, even mice!
It dissolves their insides with its venom
and then sucks them dry.
Tarantulas often live up to twenty years.

Scuba Diving Spider!

Look carefully at this underwater scene.
You'll find pond weeds, a snail,
a string of frog's eggs, and a fish.
And somewhere you'll see a big bubble.
What's inside of it? Could it be a spider?

It's a Fact:
This small, brownish spider spends its
whole life in the water.
It makes a bell of air by bringing smaller
bubbles into the water one by one.
It lives inside the "bell," swimming out
from time to time to grab a meal.

What's Behind That Trapdoor?

There's a trapdoor on the floor of this forest.
It's hidden so well you can hardly see it.
But if you look closely, you'll see a spider
peering out of the door.
Can you see its eyes?
Do you see what it's hiding from?

It's a Fact:
The trap-door spider digs a hole
using spiny teeth on its jaws.
Then it lines the hole with spider silk
and makes a secret door at the top.
From this safe tunnel,
it scoots out to catch a meal
or pops in to hide from an enemy.

Daddy Longlegs Everywhere!

Daddy longlegs are all over this window!
There are fourteen of them in this picture.
But two of them have lost a leg.
Can you find fourteen daddy longlegs?
Can you find two of them that have seven legs?

It's a Fact:
Daddy longlegs, or harvestmen,
are relatives of true spiders.
Like spiders, they have eight legs.
But these dads can drop a leg or two
to get away from an enemy.
P.S. Some daddy longleg spiders are moms!

Spooky Spider Halloween!

It's Halloween.
You can tell by the spooky decorations!
Look at all the plastic spiders!
But wait. Are they all plastic?
See if you can find three real spiders
in this Halloween scene.

It's a Fact:
There are more than 120,000 different
kinds of spiders (not counting the plastic ones).
They live in many different parts of the world.
They help people by eating billions
of insects a year.

Spider Show-Offs!

Look! Here are spiders from many places showing off their special skills.

Here's a wheel spider from Africa rolling along at 3 feet a second!

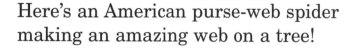

Here's an American purse-web spider making an amazing web on a tree!

Here's the bolas spider
from South America,
swinging its sticky lasso
to catch dinner!

This Australian jumping spider
with the headlight eyes is making a jump
eight times as long as its body!

This English raft spider has made a raft
to float on.

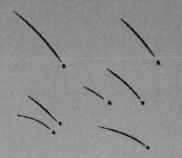

Baby spiders ballooning

House or
Sheetweb spider

Trap-door spider

Crab spider

Garden spider

Wolf spider

Bird-eating spider

Tarantula

Water spider

Ant-mimic spider

Black Widow